Sneed B. Collard III
WINGS

Illustrated by Robin Brickman

Charlesbridge

For Tessa. May your wings always carry
you where you want to go. Love, Dad

For Hillary and Dave Kilimnick and the
generation about to take wing—Robin

Boldface words can be found in the glossary at the
back of the book.

Text copyright © 2008 by Sneed B. Collard III
Illustrations copyright © 2008 by Robin Brickman
All rights reserved, including the right of reproduction in whole
or in part in any form. Charlesbridge and colophon are registered
trademarks of Charlesbridge Publishing, Inc.

Published by Charlesbridge
85 Main Street, Watertown, MA 02472
(617) 926-0329 • www.charlesbridge.com

Library of Congress Cataloging-in-Publication Data
Collard, Sneed B.
    Wings / Sneed B. Collard III ; illustrated by Robin Brickman.
        p. cm.
    ISBN 978-1-57091-611-3 (reinforced for library use)
    ISBN 978-1-57091-612-0 (softcover)
    1. Wings—Juvenile literature. I. Brickman, Robin, ill
II. Title.
QL950.8.C65 2008
591.47'9—dc22   2007002265

Printed in China
(hc) 10 9 8 7 6 5 4 3 2 1
(sc) 10 9 8 7 6 5 4 3 2 1

The three-dimensional illustrations in this book were made
    of paper painted and sculpted by Robin Brickman.
The display type and text type are set in Monotype Dante.
Separated by Chroma Graphics, Singapore
Printed and bound by Everbest Printing Company, Ltd.,
    through Four Colour Imports, Ltd., Louisville, Kentucky
Art photographed by Gamma One, New York
Production supervision by Brian G. Walker

When you want to travel far,
And you need to get there fast,
Legs and feet won't do.
Wings are best for you.

Many animals have wings.
Insects have wings.

Ladybird Beetles

Insects are the most successful group of animals on the planet. Scientists don't even know how many different kinds there are. Biologists believe that earth is home to between three and five million species of beetles alone! Like most other insects, beetles have two pairs of wings. In beetles the front, or top, two wings have evolved into hard covers called **elytra.** Elytra protect a beetle's body, especially the delicate rear wings these ladybird beetles use to fly. They also help keep a beetle from drying out.

elytra →

Birds have wings.

Galahs

About ten thousand
species of birds live on earth. Their wings
have helped them populate almost every place you
can imagine, from steamy rain forests to the frigid
North Pole. Wings give birds huge advantages over
earthbound animals. These speedy Australian galahs
eat fallen seeds from trees and fields. When the
galahs have eaten all the seeds at one place,
their wings allow them to reach another seed source
in minutes—something that might take a
walking animal hours or days to do.

So do bats.

Gambian Epauletted Fruit Bat

Of all the world's mammals, only
one group has **evolved** wings: bats.
There are eleven hundred species of bats in the
world. Most inhabit the tropics. A few can be found as far
north as the Arctic and as far south as southern South
America. Bats eat everything from insects, birds, fish,
and frogs to pollen and fruit. Vampire bats even drink
blood. Bats' ability to fly helps people in many ways.
Bats eat mosquitoes and other insect pests. They also
pollinate the flowers of plants. Bats even spread
the seeds of trees, helping forests grow and
stay healthy.

Wings come in many styles. From large.

King Vultures

It's hard to ignore king vultures flying overhead. Their beautiful black-and-white wings reach up to six feet wide and help the birds catch rising currents of warm air called **thermals.** By riding thermals, king vultures can cruise huge areas of forest for food while barely flapping their wings at all. King vultures live from central Mexico to northern Argentina. Like other vultures, they help clean up the landscape by eating dead animals, or carrion.

To small.

Bee Hummingbird

Bee hummingbirds are the world's smallest birds. They weigh less than a penny and can perch on the tip of a pencil. It's no surprise how they got their name. These birds are so small that people often mistake them for bees. Bee hummingbirds live only in Cuba. Like other hummingbirds, they use their wings to hover while they feed on the nectar of flowers. Their wings may be tiny, but they work hard, beating eighty times each second—so fast you can't even see them!

From brightly colored.

Madagascan Sunset Moth

Everyone knows butterflies display vivid colors, but so do some moths. One of the most colorful is the Madagascan sunset moth. This moth lives on the island of Madagascar in Africa. Unlike many other moths, it is active mostly in the daytime. The caterpillar, or larva, of the Madagascan sunset moth feeds on poisonous plants. The adult moth's bright colors probably warn predators, "I taste terrible, so leave me alone." Unfortunately, these same colors make the moth a target of human insect collectors. Some people even used to make jewelry out of its brightly colored wings.

Female Black Lemur

To no color at all.

Clearwing Butterflies

Although the colors of butterfly and moth wings often stand out, many of these insects' wings are camouflaged to look like dead leaves, tree trunks, and plants. Some of the most unusual wings belong to the clearwing butterflies of the American tropics. As transparent as glass, these see-through wings make the butterflies difficult to follow when they are flying. Many clearwing butterflies are poisonous, so the colored edges and veins of their wings may warn predators to stay away.

Resplendent Quetzal

Wings can be covered with feathers.

Archaeopteryx

Light feathers help provide birds with the lift they need to get off the ground. But where did feathers and birds come from? Most **paleontologists**—people who study fossils—believe that feathered birds evolved from a group of dinosaurs. At first, feathers probably kept these dinosaurs warm or helped them show off to other dinosaurs. Eventually, feathers allowed certain dinosaurs—and modern birds—to fly. Scientists believe that Archaeopteryx was the first true bird. It took flight about 150 million years ago in what is now Germany.

insect scales
up close

Scales.

Different wing patterns help butterflies and moths attract
mates, hide from predators, and even warm up in the sun.
What makes these incredible patterns? Thousands of tiny scales
on the insects' wings. The scales create color in two ways.
Many scales work like prisms, bending and separating sunlight
to create color. Scales, though, also have pigments that give
them colors. With their remarkable scales,
butterflies and moths have evolved
an almost endless variety of spots,
stripes, bands, and other
useful patterns.

Or bare, soft skin.

Lyle's Flying Foxes

Flying foxes are the world's largest bats. Some have wingspans of up to six feet. Every evening in Asia, Australia, and Africa, and on many Pacific islands, huge colonies of flying foxes take flight to look for ripe fruit and nectar to eat. Their wings may have a few fine hairs on them, but they are mostly just skin and bones. A flying fox's flexible, soft skin easily bends and folds during flight. Its huge, soft wings also make a nice shelter during the day when the bat is roosting in a mangrove tree.

But whatever they look like, most wings have one thing in common. Wings allow animals to FLY!

To fly, an animal has to create two forces: **lift** and **thrust.** Lift raises an object off the ground. Thrust moves it forward, or from place to place.

How are lift and thrust created?

In flying animals, the movement of wings create both lift and thrust. Most people think an animal's wings flap up and down, but that's not true. Wings move up, down, forward, and backward.

As wings move, air passes over and under them. Air flowing over the top of a curved wing follows a longer path than the air below. This means that the air on top gets thinner, creating less pressure than the thicker air below. When this happens, the thicker air pushes up, generating lift. Similar pressure differences—also created by the flapping of wings—generate thrust, moving the animal forward.

Common Loon

Some animals can hover in place or fly backward. How? Their wings move in complex motions, generating forces in many directions. Hummingbird and dragonfly wings, for instance, move up and down in a figure eight pattern. This maneuverability has allowed these animals to become true masters of flight.

Dragonfly

Ruby-throated
Hummingbird

17

Some wings fly fast.

Peregrine Falcon

Falcons hunt other birds and insects. To do this they have to be able to twist and turn on a dime. More important, they have to be fast. Falcons are earth's fastest flying animals. Their long wings are powered by huge flying muscles that can generate astonishing thrust. In level flight, peregrine falcons can reach speeds of sixty-five miles per hour. When they tuck in their wings and dive in a **stoop,** peregrines can top two hundred miles per hour—more than fast enough to overtake and catch almost any other kind of bird.

Others, nice and slow.

California Leaf-nosed Bat

Unlike birds, bats can change the curvature, or **camber,** of their wings. By doing so, bats can get a lot of lift out of each wing stroke and fly very slowly. The California leaf-nosed bat looks almost lazy as it flaps over the ground, but its slow flight gives the bat time to see and hear nearby prey. When it spots a grasshopper or June beetle, or hears a caterpillar's munching jaws, the bat swoops in to snag its reward.

Cricket

Wings fly short distances.

Eurasian Milkweed Bugs

Wings allow birds, bats, and insects an easy way to **migrate** when seasons change or food supplies run out. However, not all winged animals migrate long distances. Every fall Eurasian milkweed bugs fly only a few hundred yards, from milkweed patches to nearby stone outcrops or old buildings. The bugs spend the cold winter in these warmer, protected places. In spring they fly back to their favorite milkweed patches. Here the Eurasian milkweed bugs feed, mate, and lay eggs for a new generation of "mini-migrants."

And from pole to pole.

Arctic Tern

Of course, some migrating animals do fly long distances. Certain bats, butterflies, and birds migrate thousands of miles. Without a doubt, the champion of all flying migrants is the Arctic tern. Arctic terns breed in the far reaches of the Northern Hemisphere. In fall they avoid winter by flying more than twelve thousand miles to the food-rich waters of South America, southern Africa, and Antarctica. Here they stuff themselves on fish until March, when they return to the north for another breeding cycle.

Animals can have four wings.

Dragonfly

Most insects have four wings, arranged in two pairs. In moths and many other insects, these pairs are hooked or joined so they flap together. But in dragonflies the two pairs of wings operate independently. This allows dragonflies to perform amazing acrobatics as they hunt down gnats, flies, and other insect prey. Dragonflies can even hover and can fly backward. They can reach speeds of up to thirty miles per hour.

Or a single pair.

Phantom Crane Fly

Though most insects have four wings, some have only two. True flies, such as mosquitoes, gnats, and midges, have lost their second pair of wings. In these insects, the second pair of wings has evolved into tiny bumps called **halteres.** The halteres act as little **gyroscopes,** or stabilizers, that allow the insects to fly upright and straight, even in complete darkness. Other flying insects must depend on their eyesight and light to keep them from "tipping over."

23

They can use wings to chase.

Macaroni Penguins

Penguins are birds that use their wings to fly, but not through air. Instead they "fly" through water. Scientists believe that penguins evolved from other flying birds at least sixty million years ago. Today there are seventeen penguin species, and they are all super swimmers. They zoom through the water, chasing fish and shrimplike krill. The largest penguins, emperor penguins, can dive down more than seventeen hundred feet and stay underwater for eighteen minutes on a single breath.

To find mates.

Australian Regent Birds

The Australian regent bird is a kind of bower bird. Most male bower birds attract mates by building displays of sticks, called bowers, that they decorate with brightly colored objects. However, the male Australian regent bird builds sloppy little bowers. Sometimes it doesn't bother to build a bower at all! If you look at the bird's wings, you'll see why. Its brilliant yellow-and-black colors provide all the dazzle the male needs to attract a passing female.

To catch.

Little Brown Bat

Many bats use their wings to chase insect prey. But some bats also use their wings as catcher's mitts. When it gets close to a moth or other insect, this little brown bat swipes at the insect and corrals it with its wings. Then the little brown bat guides its prey to its mouth. Bats truly are wonderful insect catchers. Some bats can catch six hundred mosquitoes in a single hour! Many people who once feared bats are now helping them by putting up bat houses for these "pest controllers" to live in.

Salt Marsh Moth

Red Bat

And to flee.

Tiger Moth

Bats hunt by sight and sound, but many also locate prey by **echolocation.** Using echolocation, bats make sounds and then listen to their echoes as they bounce off nearby objects, including insect prey. But some moths—such as this tiger moth—can detect the faint sounds a bat makes. When it hears a bat's echolocation, the moth turns and flies out of range. If a bat comes too close, the moth folds its wings and dives to the ground to escape.

A few animals shed their wings.

African Termites

Termites live in huge colonies, usually underground. Most of the members of the colony are wingless. However, at certain times of year—or when a colony gets too big—some members sprout wings. These termites erupt like smoke from the colony's nest. A male and female mate and fly to a new place. Then the couple sheds its wings and settles down to become the queen and king of a new termite colony.

Or have lost them over the years.

Kiwis

Kiwis are flightless birds that live only in New Zealand. The kiwi's ancestors were flying birds with fully formed wings. New Zealand, though, had very few predators that kiwis needed to fly away from. Over millions of years, the need to fly grew smaller, along with the kiwi's wings. Today the kiwi's wings have shrunk down to two-inch nubs that are hidden under its feathers. When the bird needs to go somewhere, it simply walks or runs, relying on its dark camouflage colors to protect it.

But all in all,
Most would agree,
That wings
Are mighty useful things. . . .

Just because humans aren't born with wings doesn't
mean we don't want to fly. For thousands of years,
humans tried different ways to fly. All of them failed.
Then, in the early 1900s, the Wright brothers and
other inventors finally discovered the secrets of
flight. They built the first airplanes that could carry
human beings. What did the Wright brothers use?
Wings, of course!

Just look at our own!

Today our wings still are not as graceful as the wings of birds, bats, and insects. In fact, for an airplane's wings to generate lift, the plane needs powerful engines to push the plane forward. Still, our modern aircraft are very useful. They allow us to travel, send mail and freight, and provide emergency medical services to remote locations—all in a remarkably short time.

Resources

Arnold, Caroline. *Birds: Nature's Magnificent Flying Machines*. Watertown, MA: Charlesbridge, 2003.

Bat World Sanctuary
www.batworld.org
Learn bat facts, play bat games, and find out how to adopt a bat in order to help rehabilitate injured and orphaned bats.

Collard, Sneed B., III. *Beaks!* Watertown, MA: Charlesbridge, 2002.

Collard, Sneed B., III. *Birds of Prey: A Look at Daytime Raptors*. New York: Franklin Watts, 1999.

Cornell Lab of Ornithology
www.birds.cornell.edu
Find out more about feeding and attracting birds by watching them on live webcams.

Kalman, Bobbie. *Butterflies and Moths*. New York: Crabtree, 1994.

Latimer, Jonathan P., and Karen Stray Nolting. *Backyard Birds* (Peterson Field Guides for Young Naturalists). Boston: Houghton Mifflin, 1999.

Latimer, Jonathan P., and Karen Stray Nolting. *Songbirds* (Peterson Field Guides for Young Naturalists). Boston: Houghton Mifflin, 2000.

National Audubon Society
www.audubon.org
Discover interesting bird facts and learn how you can help birds in your own backyard.

Patent, Dorothy Hinshaw. *The Bald Eagle Returns*. Boston: Houghton Mifflin, 2000.

Pringle, Laurence. *Bats!: Strange and Wonderful*. Honesdale, PA: Boyd's Mills Press, 2000.

Pringle, Laurence. *Dragon in the Sky: The Story of a Green Darner Dragonfly*. New York: Scholastic, 2001.

The Peregrine Fund
www.peregrinefund.org
Learn about raptors and how they capture prey.

The Science Spot: World of Insects
http://sciencespot.net/Pages/kdzinsect.html
Find out everything you wanted to know about insects through these fun weblinks.

Glossary

camber (KAM-bur) The arch or curve of a wing.

echolocation (eh-koh-loh-KAY-shun) A method of hunting and navigation used by bats and some marine mammals. These animals make sounds and then listen to the returning echoes. This allows the animals to detect prey and other surrounding objects.

elytra (EH-lye-truh) The hard outer shells of beetles. Elytra protect the more delicate rear wings that are used for flight.

evolve (ee-VOLV) To change over time. Evolution is the process that allows animal and plant species to change and new species to form.

gyroscopes (JYE-ruh-skohpz) Instruments used to maintain balance in any position even when the vehicle or body they are in moves or changes position.

halteres (HAWL-tirz) The reduced second pair of wings in flies and related insects that have evolved into little nubs. Halteres help these insects stabilize themselves while in flight.

lift (LIFT) The upward force that opposes the pull of gravity in order to carry an animal or aircraft higher.

migrate (MYE-grayt) To travel from one place to another along a regular route and at a predictable time to obtain food or other resources.

paleontologist (pay-lee-awn-TAW-luh-jist) A scientist who studies ancient life by researching fossil evidence.

stoop (STOOP) The steep dive of a bird, usually to attack prey. To dive steeply [verb].

thermals (THUR-mulz) Upward currents formed by heated air rising from the earth.

thrust (THRUST) A force that creates sideways or forward motion.